YEAR 5

READING

NAPLAN*-FORMAT PRACTICE TESTS
with answers

Essential preparation for Year 5
NAPLAN* Tests in Reading

ALFRED FLETCHER

CORONEOS PUBLICATIONS

* These tests have been produced by Coroneos Publications independently of Australian
governments and are not officially endorsed publications of the NAPLAN program

Year 5 READING
NAPLAN*-FORMAT PRACTICE TESTS with answers
© Alfred Fletcher 2010
Published by Coroneos Publications 2010

ISBN 978-1-921565-48-9

* These tests have been produced by Coroneos Publications independently of Australian governments and are not officially endorsed publications of the NAPLAN program

THIS BOOK IS AVAILABLE FROM RECOGNISED BOOKSELLERS OR CONTACT:

Coroneos Publications
Telephone: (02) 9624 3 977   Facsimile: (02) 9624 3717
Business Address: 6/195 Prospect Highway Seven Hills 2147
Postal Address: PO Box 2 Seven Hills 2147
Website: www. coroneos.com.au or www.basicskillsseries.com
E-mail: coroneospublications@westnet.com.au

Contents

NOTE:

• Students have 50 minutes to complete a test.

• Students must use 2B or HB pencils only.

The NAPLAN* Test

NAPLAN* is an acronym representing the **National Assessment Program for Literacy and Numeracy**. The tests are conducted in May each year to determine the Literacy and Numeracy skills of students in Australian schools. Controversially, the results have been used by the authorities to benchmark schools on the distribution of these skills amonst students of those schools.

The tests are conducted in Year 3, Year 5, Year 7 and Year 9. The assessment program involves students completing four separate tests, in four 40 to 45 minute sessions.

The separate tests are:

- Writing: Students write a narrative in a 40 minute session.

- Reading: Each student is given a 6 or 8 page stimulus book and completes a test comprising 35 to 40 multiple choice questions.

- Language Conventions: This is atest of spelling, grammar and sentence structure.

- Numeracy : A test consisting of multiple choice or short answer questions in numeracy (mathematics). In year 7 and Year 9 students answer **non-calculator** and **calculator allowed** questions in separate parts of the test.

This book is designed to help you practise for the the NAPLAN* tests and develop the skills necessary to competently handle any task presented to you at this stage of your development.

* The practice tests in this book have been produced by Five Senses Education Pty Ltd

   independently of Australian governments and are not officially endorsed publications of the

   NAPLAN program

The Reading Task

This book is designed to help you practise for the Reading section of the NAPLAN* test and develop the skills necessary to competently handle any reading task presented to you at this stage of your development. The NAPLAN* test in reading examines your ability to read texts and understand what you have read. Practicing these will develop skills that will assist you in all areas of your reading and comprehension.

Also included in this book are some hints on how to improve your reading and comprehension skills. Follow these hints and use them in your work as they may assist you in gaining additional vital marks under examination conditions. They will also help you develop your overall English skills and benefit your work in general.

We wish you all the best for the exam and know that the activities and tasks in this book will assist you in reaching your reading potential.

The NAPLAN* test includes a reading task which asks you to read a variety of texts that are similar to the things you read in the classroom. These texts are in the form of a 'Reading Magazine' which usually contains, in Year 5 SIX pages of texts that you will have to read and understand. This magazine is TWELVE pages long by Year Nine. There is also a title page and a back page which has the sample text on it. This last page is not part of the exam. This magazine is in colour and the graphics or pictures can help you understand the story. No questions are asked specifically on the graphics.

The other section of the reading task is a booklet of questions that asks you about each of the six texts you have read in the 'Reading Magazine'. These questions test your ability to understand and comprehend what you have read. You have to 'shade the bubble' to record your answer although in some questions you are asked to number the boxes to show the order of events in the text. Sample questions are provided at the end of this section to give an indication of the type of questions that you might encounter in this book and in the test.

What Markers Look For When Examining Your Work

Of course your test will be marked and so it is good to know what the examiner or marker is looking for. The examiner is looking to test your ability to read different types of texts such as factual texts, stories and as you get older things like letters, posters, poetry and reviews. All the questions are based on the work you have been doing in class and there is no penalty for incorrect answers. The difficulty of the questions will vary from straightforward comprehension to more complex understanding and comparative questions.

Each year the examination tests the skill and developmental areas appropriate to the level being tested. In Year 5 for example the test might, in one year, test your ability to find information, connect ideas, come to conclusions, find the main purpose of a text, compare differing points of view and show your understanding of a character, what they do and why they do it.

In some ways the reading test is also a test of vocabulary and how well you know complex vocabulary and are able to interpret it. I cannot emphasise enough the worth of developing a good vocabulary as it will help you in all areas of every subject that you will be asked to do during your education.

The reading section is reported similarly to the other areas, that is, in bands with Band 10 being the highest in Year Nine, Band 9 in Year 7, Band 8 in Year 5 and Band 6 in Year 3. Similarly the bottom Bands change according to Year with Band 1 the lowest skill level in Year 3.

In this section you do not have to write sentence responses just shade bubbles or write numbers. You will be expected to answer all the questions and select one bubble from the four choices (usually) provided in the question. If you make a mistake put a X through the bubble and shade the bubble you now think the answer should be.

By understanding clearly the information you have just read you will have taken the first major step on your path to success in these tests. By knowing what you have to do you will be prepared for it and confident in what you need to do to succeed. Re-read these introductory notes several times. Then you know what to expect in the exam and won't be surprised by the words in the exam or the format. Practice questions such as those in this book make you familiar with the language and format of the paper. The next section gives you some reading and comprehension tips to help improve your ability to reach your potential in the exam.

IMPROVING YOUR READING AND COMPREHENSION SKILLS

Reading improvement is a matter of practice and developing your skills and understanding so you can comprehend the text(s) you are reading. There are some simple things you can do to build your skills in this area.

Read as Widely as You Can and With Purpose.

The best way to improve your reading skills is to read. This doesn't have to be books but might be magazines, newspapers, pamphlets, anything really that will develop your ability to learn words. As you read you will meet words that you don't know – this is a great opportunity to grab a dictionary or ask someone what that word means and add it to your vocabulary. The wider your vocabulary the better your understanding will be and you can then read more difficult texts. Vocabulary is one of the keys to understanding. Use a library for free reading materials.

Read Different Text Types.

By reading and knowing the different text types you will be more confident when going into any activity in any subject, not just the exam. Try to read more than narrative texts try reading recounts, expositions, procedures, descriptions and discussions for example. As you get older you will read poetry, biography and reviews as well. Try and read for at least 20 minutes a day and more as you get older.

Learn Simple Literary Devices

As you get older you will need to recognise more than paragraphs, sentences and the simple parts of sentences. As you read you will be required to recognise and understand simple literary devices such as similes and synonyms and be able to understand why they are used. As a reader you will also be asked to understand the different levels of meaning in a text (literal, inferential and evaluative).

Develop Your Skills through Practise and Repetition

You have already taken one step by reading this book. To be a higher order reader you need to be able to predict in your reading and be able to identify and discuss different text types and identify bias and point of view in a text. One of the final stages is to be able to question or even challenge what the writer is saying after reflecting on the material. To be able to do these things you need to practise your skills at different levels.

The secret here is to keep testing yourself on harder texts and question types once you have mastered the level you are on. Don't push yourself harder than this. There is no point going to the next level if you haven't understood all the reading at the level you are on. Reading without comprehending what you are reading is frustrating. Go back and gain confidence with what you can do.

Now it is time to try some questions and see how you go.

Sample Questions

Read the following story and answer the four questions on the next page. You will find these questions similar to the types you will find in this book and the examination.

URBAN LEGENDS

THE LEGEND:

It was once a common among parents holidaying in Florida to bring back baby alligators for their children to have as pets. These infant alligators eventually grew up and became to big to handle. This caused a disposal problem. Their desperate owners flushed them down the toilet or released them into the sewers/ stormwater to get rid of them.

Some of these speedily disposed-of creatures managed to survive and breed in the dark city sewer system, so the story goes, producing colonies of giant, albino alligators beneath the streets of New York. Their babies thrive down there to this day, completely hidden except for the rare scary encounter between sewer gator and underground worker.

Is this the truth or just an urban myth? What do you think?

1 **Why did parents bring back baby alligators?**
○ to put in the sewer
○ to donate to the zoo
○ to keep as children's pets
○ to remind them of Florida

2 **Another word for "infant' in the passage might be?**
○ crocodile
○ baby
○ reptile
○ small

3 **What colour did the underground alligators turn?**
○ albino
○ brown
○ green
○ lemon

4 **Write the numbers 1 to 4 in the spaces to show the order events happen in the legend**
_____ alligators bred underground
_____ alligators arrive from Florida
_____ alligators are dumped when growing
_____ alligators meet underground workers

Answers
1 to keep as children's pets
2 baby
3 albino
4 alligators arrive from Florida,
alligators dumped when growing,
alligators bred underground,
alligators met underground workers.

End of Sample Questions
To complete the rest of the questions in this book you will need to refer to the
Year 5 Naplan Format Reading Magazine

READING TEST 1

Stimulus 1

Read the story about *Castles* on page 2 of the reading magazine and answer the following questions.

1 **Castles were built by?**

Shade one bubble

○ lords and nobles

○ lords, nobles and the rich

○ kings and nobles

○ lords, nobles and kings

2 **Castles were built to?**

○ protect the countryside

○ protect people and stock

○ protect the moat

○ protect the king

3 **The words earth and timber refer to?**

○ defences

○ building materials

○ castles

○ kings, lords and nobles

4 **Why did castles go out of favour?**

○ stone walls

○ gunpowder

○ hard to defend

○ too cold

5   According to the information what are castles being used for now?

○ renovation

○ great views

○ historic value

○ homes

6   Another accurate title for this story could be

○ Short History of Castles

○ Castles and War

○ Castles and Animals

○ Sand Castles

Stimulus 2

Read the story about *Rubbish and You* on page 4 of the reading magazine and answer the following questions.

7   Why is the problem of rubbish greater now?

○ too much junk thrown out

○ number of people on the planet

○ not enough rubbish bins

○ rubbish has become more dangerous

8   Who is trying to educate people about rubbish?

○ town councils

○ environmental groups

○ garbage collectors

○ many people

9 **Which word is a synonym for rubbish?**

○ refuse

○ recycle

○ landfill

○ collection

10 **The purpose of this article is?**

○ to explain the dangers of rubbish and avoid them

○ to explain rubbish and how you can help

○ to list all the rubbish in the world and its effect

○ to state how rubbish is created and how we stop it

11 **The word reduces in the article can also mean?**

○ small

○ lessen

○ enlarge

○ never

12 **How can you help the problem?**

○ don't create rubbish

○ find new landfill sites

○ don't buy anything

○ dispose of rubbish thoughtfully

Stimulus 3

Read the story about *Kenny's Big Day Out* on page 6 of the reading magazine and answer the following questions.

13 **Kenny's aim on his big day out was to?**
- ○ catch people dumping waste
- ○ walk slowly down to the creek
- ○ lie on the sandy bank and read
- ○ catch tadpoles and paddle in the water

14 **The men he saw were?**
- ○ all named Mick and Keith
- ○ wearing strange greyish suits
- ○ chasing him through the water
- ○ dumping fluids into the creek

15 **The first paragraph Kenny turned down the familiar... is mainly about?**
- ○ dangers to the environment
- ○ Kenny's plans for his big day out
- ○ bushwalking safely near creeks
- ○ seeing the pollution in the creek

16 **"Get the kid!" is an example of?**
- ○ dialogue
- ○ questioning
- ○ plot
- ○ discussion

17 Why would the men want to "get" Kenny?

  ◯ so he wouldn't report their activities

  ◯ because they wanted to have some fun

  ◯ so they could get him to help them

  ◯ because they wanted Kenny in a drum

18 Write the numbers 1 to 4 in the spaces to show the order events happen in the story

  _____ Kenny saw the men polluting the creek

  _____ Kenny saw the pollution in the creek

  _____ Kenny slipped as he was watching the men

  _____ Kenny turned down the track

Stimulus 4   AUSTRALIAN WILDLIFE

Read the story on page 8 of the reading magazine and answer the following questions.

19 Two words in paragraph one that tell us Australian animals are unique are?

  ◯ amazed and loved

  ◯ rare and unusual

  ◯ gentle and loved

  ◯ rare and gentle

20 Koalas feed on?

  ◯ all sorts of eucalyptus leaves

  ◯ eucalyptus trees and branches

  ◯ twelve varieties of eucalyptus leaves

  ◯ roots, grass and leaves

21 Wombats have no enemies because?

- ◯ they are large and live in burrows
- ◯ wombats are vegetarian so nothing eats them
- ◯ they are large, muscular and have large claws
- ◯ wombats have large claws and are solid

22 A fact about the platypus is?

- ◯ they live for over twelve years
- ◯ they can eat more than their bodyweight in a day
- ◯ the male platypus has a poisonous spur
- ◯ platypus feed in the early morning

23 The word endangered in the passage is closest in meaning to?

- ◯ at risk
- ◯ safeguard
- ◯ dangerous
- ◯ enamoured

24 The sentence 'You might think of others!' asks you to?

- ◯ think about endangered Australian animals
- ◯ think about kangaroos and emus
- ◯ think about other unique Australian animals
- ◯ thinks about how these animals will survive

Stimulus 5   Zalika's Trial

Read the extract from the novel *Zalika and the Gods of Wroth* by Uriah Heep on page 10 of the reading magazine and answer the following questions.

25 The author of this story is?

○ Zalika

○ Briannon

○ Hensley

○ Heep

26 Briannon is dripping in the story?

○ because she is sweating with fear

○ because she has swum the River Wroth

○ because she has walked through a waterfall

○ because the cave is dripping

27 'Today is only yesterday's tomorrow' is a?

○ saying

○ moral

○ inscription

○ instruction

28 The words 'black as pitch' are an example of?

○ repetition

○ adverb

○ simile

○ sentence

29 Another word for 'aloft' in the passage might be?

○ ahead

○ brightness

○ rays

○ above

30 Two people who have helped Zalika are?

○ Briannon and Wroth

○ Briannon and The Traveller in Time

○ Hensley and The Circle of Hands

○ The Traveller in Time and Wroth

31 This excerpt is an example of a?

○ recount

○ narrative

○ discussion

○ report

Stimulus 6

Read the story about *Androcles* on page 12 of the reading magazine and answer the following questions.

32 The phrase 'he turned to flee' means?

○ the lion tried to escape

○ Androcles was going to run

○ Androcles ran away to safety

○ the lion moved to chase Androcles

33 In the story the lion is compared to a?

○ lion

○ emperor

○ court

○ dog

34 In the story the words "bound up" mean?

○ Androcles tied the lion up

○ Androcles was tied up by the Emperor

○ Androcles fixed the lions wound

○ Androcles was imprisoned

35 The lion was kept without food for several days?

○ to make it hungry and vicious

○ to make it angry

○ to make it thinner as it was fat

○ to make its paw hurt again

36 Another word for 'fawned' in the passage might be?

○ brown

○ servile

○ deer

○ angry

37 A moral is?

○ a short sentence that tells the lesson of the story

○ a short sentence that gives a lesson

○ a short sentence that should be the title

○ a short sentence that uses complex vocabulary

38 **Write the numbers 1 to 4 in the spaces to show the order events happen in the story**

_____ Androcles pulls the thorn from the lions paw.

_____ Androcles is sent to the arena

_____ Androcles escaped from his master

_____ Androcles is pardoned

END OF READING TEST 1

READING TEST 2

Stimulus 7

Read the story about *Cavies* on page 14 of the reading magazine and answer the following questions

Shade one bubble

1   **Another name for cavies is?**
○ Peruvian
○ Guinea pig
○ Europe
○ Smooth-haired

2   **A country found in South America is?**
○ Abyssinian
○ Europe
○ Peru
○ South America

3   **The words Peruvian, Smooth-haired and Abyssinian refer to?**
○ breeds of cavy
○ colours of cavies
○ foods of cavies
○ types of cavies

4   **Two foods cavies dislike are?**
○ onions and chaff
○ rhubarb and potatoes
○ rhubarb and pellets
○ rabbit pellets and hay

5 According to the information cavies are good pets because they?

 ○ are gentle, quiet and safe

 ○ come in any colour desired

 ○ are not pigs but rodents

 ○ are easy to feed

6 Another accurate title for this story could be?

 ○ Cavies through History

 ○ Cavies and Me

 ○ Cavies as Pets

 ○ Cavies: Legend from South America

Stimulus 8

Read the story about *Erosion* on page 15 of the reading magazine and answer the following questions

7 Two causes of erosion are?

 ○ wind and animals

 ○ plants and animals

 ○ wind and trees

 ○ housing and land

8 Land erodes more quickly if it has?

 ○ been left untouched

 ○ been left in the wind

 ○ been affected by humans

 ○ once been a creek

9 **Which word is a synonym for damaging?**

○ creative

○ harmful

○ carefully

○ disrepair

10 **The purpose of this article is?**

○ to show how erosion is caused by humans

○ to explain erosion and some ways to stop it

○ to list all the causes of erosion on the planet

○ to explain the problem of erosion

11 **The word normal in the article can also mean?**

○ sound

○ complex

○ natural

○ basic

12 **What are two ways to help the problem of erosion?**

○ planting trees and recycling

○ stop building houses and factories

○ stop animals burrowing and plant trees

○ planting trees and building terraces

Stimulus 9

Read the storis about _Hercules_, on page 16 of the reading magazine and answer the following questions

13 Hercules was a hero in which mythology?

- ○ Roman
- ○ Norse
- ○ Greek
- ○ Nemean

14 How was the Nemean Lion protected?

- ○ it was supernatural and old
- ○ its skin could not be penetrated
- ○ it had a huge roar and scared people
- ○ it lived in a cave that was hard to find

15 The first paragraph 'As his first labour...' is mainly about?

- ○ the Hydra
- ○ Hercules childhood
- ○ the Supernatural
- ○ the Nemean Lion

16 'As soon as one head is beaten down or chopped off, ... is an example of?

- ○ simile
- ○ questioning
- ○ dialogue
- ○ discussion

17 **Lerna in the story is where?**

○ the Hydra lived

○ Hercules lived

○ the Nemean Lion lived

○ the storytellers lived

18 **Write the numbers 1 to 4 in the spaces to show the order events happen in the story**

_____ Hercules crawled into the cave

_____ Hercules wore the lion's skin

_____ Hercules' friend helped him

_____ Hercules was challenged to kill the lion

Stimulus 10

Read the story entitled *Jungle Escape* on page 18 of the reading magazine and answer the following questions

19 **The two words in paragraph one that explain Kestrin's terrible situation are?**

○ pack prowling

○ jungle lore

○ no wood

○ dangerous predicament

20 **Kestrin is hiding in the cave from?**

○ the Park Ranger

○ a pack of hyenas

○ white bones

○ the African jungle

21 **Kestrin knew she had little time because?**

○ it was getting dark outside

○ the fire was burning slowly

○ the pack howled in fury

○ the hyenas were very hungry

22 **A fact about Kestrin is?**

○ she is afraid of the dark and hyenas

○ she will not escape from the cave

○ she is twelve years old and lives in the jungle

○ she has a Park Ranger for a father

23 **The word intensity in the passage is closest in meaning to?**

○ keenness

○ lifeline

○ savagery

○ calamity

24 **The phrase 'white bones of other victims' suggests you to?**

○ hyenas had died in the cave

○ the hyenas had killed here before

○ other animals lived in the cave

○ Kestrin saw a ghost

Stimulus 11

Read the storis about *The Savannah* on page 19 of the reading magazine and answer the following questions

25 **The savannah habitat is generally made up of?**
○ grasses and unique animals
○ coarse grasses and scattered trees
○ scattered trees and big animals
○ coarse grasses and prey

26 **Animals that migrate have?**
○ burrows and wings
○ long wings and short legs
○ long legs or wings
○ unique qualities such as long necks

27 **Savannah animals burrow because?**
○ they are avoiding the heat
○ raising their young
○ avoiding the heat or raising young
○ they are avoiding birds of prey

28 **The words 'never, never' are an example of?**
○ repetition
○ adverb
○ simile
○ sentence

29 Another word for 'predators' in the passage might be?

- ⬭ ranger
- ⬭ traverse
- ⬭ stealth
- ⬭ hunters

30 Elephants are rarely attacked because?

- ⬭ they live in large groups and eat trees
- ⬭ they have thick grey skin and are very big
- ⬭ they are the biggest animals on earth
- ⬭ they taste like grass and have big ears

31 This excerpt is an example of a?

- ⬭ recount
- ⬭ narrative
- ⬭ discussion
- ⬭ report

Stimulus 12

Read the story about *Timmy to the Rescue* on page 20 of the reading magazine and answer the following questions

32   'What about a swim in the river' is a?

○ statement

○ exclamation

○ question

○ sentence

33   In the story the boys see the burglars when?

○ they are building the hideout

○ collecting logs in the forest

○ sitting in the river

○ lunching in Windsor Hall

34   In the story the phrase 'filling the van with valuables' mean?

○ the thieves van was full of cheap items

○ the burglars had a valuable, well appointed van

○ the burglars were putting stolen goods in the van

○ the thieves had stolen the van and could sell it

25   The Richman family had gone on holidays to?

○ the south of France

○ Windsor Hall

○ the riverbank

○ The Ancient Woods

36 Another word for 'investigate' in the passage might be?

○ forget

○ enquire

○ trek

○ search

37 Why does Timmy run for the forest at the end of the story?

○ he wants to hide the keys

○ he wants to get to the hideout quickly

○ he is heading for the police station

○ he has been spotted by the burglars

38 Write the numbers 1 to 4 in the spaces to show the order events happen in the story

_____ The three boys are building a hideout.

_____ The boys go to investigate

_____ The boys sneak around the stables

_____ Timmy suggests they go to the river

END OF READING TEST 2

READING TEST 3

Stimulus 13.

Read the story about the *Goldfish* on page 21 of the reading booklet and answer the following questions.

1 **Who first kept goldfish as pets?**

Shade one bubble

○ Goldfish

○ Japanese

○ Australians

○ Chinese

2 **What colours does the goldfish come in?**

○ red, black and white

○ gold, red and black

○ red, black, white and green

○ gold, red, black and white

3 **Goldfish live for over?**

○ two years

○ five years

○ ten years

○ twenty years

4 **Pellets and flakes are?**

○ goldfish foods

○ fish tank foods

○ rabbit foods

○ tank decorations

5 According to the information goldfish have how many varieties?

- ○ two
- ○ four
- ○ five
- ○ ten

6 Another accurate title for this story could be?

- ○ My Pets
- ○ Fish Fingers
- ○ Keeping Fish
- ○ The History of the Goldfish

Stimulus 14.

Read the story about *Blackbeard* on page 22 of the reading booklet and answer the following questions.

7 Blackbeard's real name was?

- ○ Blackbeard Teach
- ○ Edward teach
- ○ Edward Blackbeard
- ○ Robert Maynard

8 How did he get his pirate name?

- ○ he was a teacher before becoming a pirate
- ○ he had a huge black beard
- ○ he had a skull and cross bones for a flag
- ○ he was searching for his head

9   The third paragraph 'Outnumbered the pirates…' is mainly about?

○ how Blackbeard got his name

○ the pirate party on the island

○ Blackbeard's defeat and his ghost

○ pirate treasure and where to find it

10 The story of 'Blackbeard's Ghost' is an example of?

○ legend

○ report

○ instruction

○ description

11 What is Blackbeard's ghost searching for?

○ his treasure

○ his ship and crew

○ his head

○ his secret hideout

12 Write the numbers 1 to 4 in the boxes to show the order events happen in the story

_____ Blackbeard had a party at his hideaway

_____ Blackbeard was defeated by Robert Maynard

_____ Blackbeard terrorized the sailors

_____ Blackbeard's ghost searches for his head

Stimulus 15

Read the story about *Harmony Day* on page 24 of the reading magazine and answer the following questions

13 **Harmony Day is organised by?**
- ○ Department of Immigration and Citizenship
- ○ Harmony Day Committee
- ○ Department of Citizenship and Immigration
- ○ Australian Government and school groups

14 **Harmony Day promotes?**
- ○ harmony amongst peoples
- ○ Australians
- ○ belonging
- ○ cultural diversity

15 **Which word is an antonym for 'opportunity'?**
- ○ connection
- ○ restraint
- ○ juncture
- ○ convoluted

16 **The purpose of this article is?**
- ○ to explain what Harmony Day is
- ○ to explain why Harmony Day began
- ○ to list all the activities on Harmony Day
- ○ to analyse the effect of Harmony Day

17 **The word 'unite' in the article can also mean?**

○ divide

○ saturate

○ fix

○ link

18 **What are two ways that schools could be involved?**

○ selling badges and showbags

○ respecting cultures and making posters

○ organising food days or games days

○ organising games days and making posters

Stimulus 16

Read the story about *Desert Mystery* on page 25 of the reading magazine and answer the following questions

19 **The word 'struggling' suggests that?**

○ the group were enjoying the desert

○ the group were hiking and sight-seeing

○ the group were having a hard time in the desert

○ the group were close to finding the hidden oasis

20 **Toby is going out with?**

○ Jemima

○ Rocco

○ Toby

○ Stephanie

21 The story tells us the group were out of?

- ○ hope
- ○ water
- ○ fuel
- ○ sand

22 A fact in the story is?

- ○ there are no pyramids in the desert
- ○ Rocco is a pilot
- ○ the group were in a plane crash
- ○ Jemima met Tony in the desert

23 The word 'listless' in the passage is closest in meaning to?

- ○ running
- ○ lethargic
- ○ breakdown
- ○ traipse

24 The phrase 'sun blistered faces' suggests you to?

- ○ the group enjoyed sunbaking
- ○ the group was hot but happy
- ○ the group had too much sun
- ○ the sun shone on their faces

Stimulus 17

Read the story about *Football* on page 26 of the reading magazine and answer the following questions

25 Football is also known in Australia as?

○ the world game

○ the beautiful game

○ soccer

○ league

26 Football teams have how many players?

○ one

○ 1863

○ eleven

○ four

27 The goalkeeper is?

○ allowed to catch the ball in mitts

○ allowed to touch and catch the ball

○ not allowed to head and kick the ball

○ not allowed to dive quickly

28 The words 'stuck like glue' are an example of?

○ repetition

○ adverb

○ simile

○ sentence

29 Another word for 'consist' in the passage might be?

- ◯ amongst
- ◯ comprise
- ◯ deletion
- ◯ include

30 In football what occurs every four years?

- ◯ new rules are made in England
- ◯ the World Cup takes place
- ◯ new competitions are formed
- ◯ Australia competes in the World Cup

32 This excerpt is an example of a?

- ◯ discussion
- ◯ narrative
- ◯ news article
- ◯ report

Stimulus 18

Read the story about *Man Overboard* on page 27 of the reading magazine and answer the following questions

33 'the wind whipped the waves' is an example of?

○ statement

○ exclamation

○ question

○ description

34 In the story the magistrate is?

○ Richard

○ Richard's father

○ the man on the boat

○ the man on the beach

35 In the story the phrase 'bad weather made visibility poor' mean?

○ the water was very rough and choppy

○ the weather made it hard to see

○ the weather was great for beachcombing

○ the smugglers were having a good night

36 How do we know the smuggler on the beach was cowardly?

○ he could not swim

○ he was a smuggler

○ he ran away and didn't help

○ Richard saw his beady eyes

37 Another word for 'blustery' in the passage might be?

○ softly

○ reckoning

○ turbulent

○ calm

38 How does Richard help his father?

○ he arrests the cowardly smuggler

○ he sneaks out to watch his father

○ he pulls on the rope and wades out to help

○ he wants to be a magistrate like his father

39 Write the numbers 1 to 4 in the spaces to show the order events happen in the story

_____ Richard's father runs to the beach.

_____ The smuggler runs away

_____ Richard's father hid behind an outcrop

_____ Richard helps in the rescue

END OF READING TEST 3

Test 1   Answers

1   lords, nobles and kings

2   people and stock

3   building materials

4   hard to defend

5   homes

6   Short History of Castles

7   number of people on the planet

8   environmental groups

9   refuse

10   to explain rubbish and how you can help

11   lessen

12   dispose of rubbish thoughtfully

13   lie on the sandy bank and read

14   dumping fluids into the creek

15   Kenny's plans for his big day out

16   dialogue

17   so he wouldn't report their activities

18   Kenny turned down the track,
         Kenny saw the pollution in the creek,
         Kenny saw the men polluting the creek,
         Kenny slipped as he was watching the men

19	rare and unusual
20	twelve varieties of eucalyptus leaves
21	they are large, muscular and have large claws
22	the male platypus has a poisonous spur
23	at risk
24	think about other unique Australian animals
25	Heep
26	because she has walked through a waterfall
27	inscription
28	simile
29	above
30	Briannon and the Traveller in Time
31	narrative
32	Androcles was going to run
33	dog
34	Androcles fixed the lion's wound
35	to make it hungry and vicious
36	servile
37	a short sentence that tells the lesson of the story
38	Androcles escaped from his master, Androcles pulls the thorn from the lion's paw, Androcles is sent to the arena, Androcles is pardoned.

Test 2   Answers

1   Guinea pig

2   Peru

3   types of cavies

4   rhubarb and potatoes

5   are gentle, quiet and safe

6   Cavies as Pets

7   wind and animals

8   been affected by humans

9   harmful

10   to explain erosion and some ways to stop it

11   natural

12   planting trees and building terraces

13   Greek

14   Its skin could not be penetrated

15   The Nemean Lion

16   dialogue

17   the Hydra lived

18   Hercules was challenged to kill the lion,
     Hercules crawled into the cave,
     Hercules wore the lion's skin,
     Hercules' friend helped him.

19	Dangerous predicament
20	a pack of hyenas
21	the pack howled in fury
22	she has a Park Ranger for a father
23	keenness
24	the hyenas had killed here before
25	coarse grasses and scattered trees
26	long legs or wings
27	avoiding the heat or raising young
28	repetition
29	hunters
30	they have thick skin and are very big
31	report
32	question
33	sitting in the river
34	the burglars were putting stolen goods in the van
35	the south of France
36	enquire
37	he has been spotted by the burglars
38	the three boys are building a hideout, Timmy suggests they go to the river, the boys go to investigate, the boys sneak around the stables.

Test 3   Answers

1   Chinese

2   gold, red, black and white

3   ten years

4   goldfish foods

5   ten

6   Keeping Fish

7   Edward Teach

8   He had a huge black beard

9   Blackbeard's defeat and his ghost

10   legend

11   his head

12   Blackbeard terrorized the sailors,
Blackbeard had a party at his hideaway,
Blackbeard was defeated by Robert Maynard,
Blackbeard's ghost searches for his head.

13   Department of Immigration and Citizenship

14   cultural diversity

15   restraint

16   to explain what Harmony Day is

17   link

18   organising food days or games days

19	The group were having a hard time in the desert
20	Stephanie
21	water
22	the group were in a plane crash
23	lethargic
24	the group had too much sun
25	soccer
26	eleven
27	allowed to touch and catch the ball
28	simile
29	comprise
30	the World Cup takes place
31	news article
32	description
33	Richard's father
34	the weather made it hard to see
35	he ran away and didn't help
36	turbulent
37	he pulls on the rope and wades out to help
38	Richard's father hides behind an outcrop Richard's father runs to the beach, the smuggler runs away, Richard helps in the rescue.

Reading Magazine

Year 5

Stimulus One: Castles

Castles were built for over 900 years and they had many features including arrow slits and moats with drawbridges. Castles were originally built in Europe in the 9th century and used to control the surrounding countryside. A castle is a type of fort built in Europe and the Middle East a long time ago. Castles were usually built by lords, nobles and kings to protect people and stock from attackers.

Often built on hills to show power they were a gathering point for the local people. Castles were built from earth and timber, but had their defences replaced later by stone. Early castles often exploited natural defences, such as rivers and lakes or hills. The use of gunpowder made castles hard to defend and they went out of favour. Later many people wanted castles for homes and restored them.

3

Stimulus Two: RUBBISH AND YOU

Basically rubbish is the things that people don't want and it comes in many shapes and forms. It has many names such as junk, garbage, refuse and waste and people have been creating rubbish for all of time.

The problem has now become larger because of the number of people on the planet but also because we consume so much and are creating new things all the time to replace the old.

Some rubbish can be recycled such as paper, glass and some plastics. This reduces the problem of rubbish but not everything can be recycled so it has to be put somewhere. Much of it goes to the local rubbish dump or landfill site. Finding these sites has become a problem as nobody wants to live near a dump. Dumps can attract pests such as rats and create other problems such as cancerous smoke from fires and nuclear waste.

Many people are now very concerned about rubbish and how it affects our lives. Environmental groups try to educate people to use less and recycle more. You need to think about these things when you put the bins out for collection at your house. Think about what you can do to help. Rubbish makes places look messy so make sure you dispose of rubbish thoughtfully.

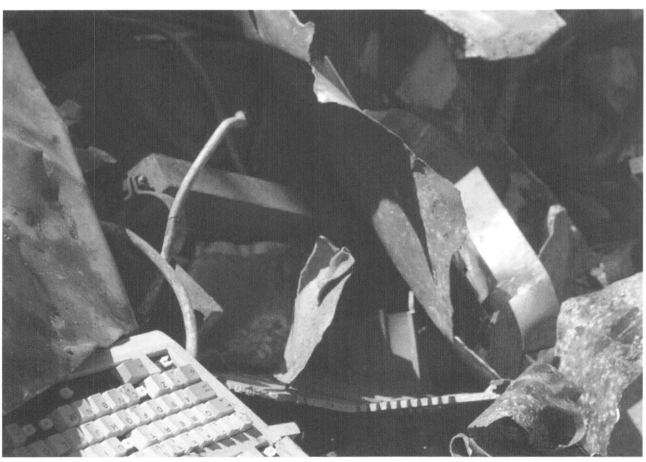

Stimulus Three: Kenny's Big Day Out

(an extract from a novel by Ruby Tuesday)

Kenny turned down the familiar track as he walked to his favourite spot on the creek. It was here that he first caught a tadpole and went paddling in the shallow water. His day had been planned for weeks and he looked forward to lying on the sandy bank and reading his favourite horror book, *Strolling Bones*. His back pack bounced gently on his back as he slid down the last dip to the bank.

What Kenny saw was not what he expected. The water was a funny grey colour and it foamed as it came into contact with the bank. Concerned Kenny moved closer and could then smell the unusual odour coming from the foam. His spot and his day were ruined and this made him cross. He decided to investigate.

Walking upstream Kenny heard a clanging noise and snuck around the big fallen eucalypt. He could see three men with strange suits on tipping fluid from drums into the creek. One had 'Mick' written on his helmet while another had 'Keith'. Moving closer Kenny was watching so intently he slipped and fell creating some noise as he cried out. The men turned and saw him. One yelled out, "Get the kid!"

Kenny bolted.

Stimulus Four: **AUSTRALIAN WILDLIFE**

Australia has many rare and unusual animals that have amazed people over time. One particularly loved animal is the Koala which sleeps for eighty percent of the day. They have a grey soft furred coat, with a white chest, flat nose and big ears, and clawed feet for climbing trees. They are very gentle animals, and do not move around a lot. Koalas feed on eucalyptus leaves, but will only munch on twelve varieties. This is also how they drink.

Another fascinating Australian animal is the platypus which lives in freshwater creeks and lakes in burrows. They move around at night to feed and can eat their own bodyweight in one day. They eat insect larvae, worms and insects and live for twelve years. The male platypus has a poisonous spur to defend itself and this can cause humans great pain. The platypus is endangered because its habitat is being destroyed.

Our final Aussie animal is the wombat which lives in burrows and has no enemies as it is so large, muscular and has large claws. They eat roots, grass and leaves. They eat through the evening and night and sleep in the day. A wombat can sleep with all four legs pointing up into the air.

These are just some of our unique Australian animals. You might think of others!

Stimulus 5: ZALIKA'S TRIAL

(an excerpt from the novel *Zalika and the Gods of Wroth* by Uriah Heep)

Zalika and Briannon were now confronted by the sacred inscription on the Tomb of Wroth having passed through the waterfall. Still dripping, Briannon read it aloud, 'Today is only yesterday's tomorrow'.

They both thought the words over very carefully but nothing came to mind and Zalika thought that she would save the words for her final trial. She would now have to leave Briannon behind as the old gypsy had told them only one could make the final part of the journey. Zalika hugged Briannon who promised to wait for her and then headed off into the cave.

The path grew narrower and darker as she entered the bowels of the earth until it was as black as pitch. Undaunted Zalika pulled out her light crystal and held it aloft to guide the way. She got the impression that whatever lay ahead for her she would have to defeat it if she was going to see another July morning. The Traveller in Time had warned her of this day but she had never realised the fear she would feel as she forged ahead.

The crystal's light was faint in the darkness and Zalika could feel the walls getting closer as if the darkness was alive. Drawing on the powers that the Circle of Hands had given her she plunged forward to meet the cause of all misery, the magician's nephew, Hensley.

Stimulus Six: Androcles

A slave named Androcles once escaped from his master and fled to the forest. As he was wandering about there he came upon a lion lying down moaning and groaning. At first he turned to flee, but finding that the lion did not pursue him, he turned back and went up to him. As he came near, the lion put out his paw, which was all swollen and bleeding, and Androcles found that a huge thorn had entered it, and was causing all the pain. He pulled out the thorn and bound up the paw of the lion, who was soon able to rise and lick the hand of Androcles like a dog. Then the lion took Androcles to his cave, and every day used to bring him meat from which to live.

Shortly afterwards both Androcles and the lion were captured, and the slave was sentenced to be thrown to the lion, after the lion had been kept without food for several days. The Emperor and all his Court came to see the spectacle, and Androcles was led out into the middle of the arena. Soon the lion was let loose from his den and rushed bounding and roaring towards his victim. But as soon as he came near to Androcles he recognised his friend, and fawned upon him, and licked his hands like a friendly dog. The Emperor, surprised at this, summoned Androcles to him, who told him the whole story. The slave was pardoned and freed, and the lion let loose in his native forest.

Moral: Gratitude is the sign of noble souls.

Stimulus 7
Cavies

Cavies or guinea pigs as they are more commonly known in Australia originally come from Peru, a country in South America. Indeed they are not really pigs either but rodents. The cavy was once a wild animal but became pets when they were transported to Europe. Perhaps their common name came from the squeaks and squeals they make to communicate.

Cavies make great pets because they are gentle, quiet and safe around children. Cavies come in three types; the Peruvian, the Smooth-haired and the Abyssinian and can be any colour. They are easy to feed and are plant eaters. They will eat cavy or rabbit pellets, chaff and some hays but they don't like mouldy grass, onion, potatoes and rhubarb.

Stimulus 8
Erosion

Erosion is the process of breaking down or weathering of solids in the natural environment and moving them to another. place. It usually occurs through wind, water or ice by washing down of soil and other material under gravity. Another cause is by living organisms, such as animals which burrow and scrape.

Erosion is a natural process, but it has been increased to a damaging level by human's use of land in activities such as housing, agriculture and clearing of forests and land. Land that has been affected by humans erodes more quickly than untouched land.

One way of stopping erosion is by planting trees and shrubs to help hold the soil together, building terraces on slopes and slowing water over bare land. A certain amount of erosion is normal and good for the environment. It moves soil from one place to another and provides new nutrients for plants and animals.

Stimulus 9
Hercules

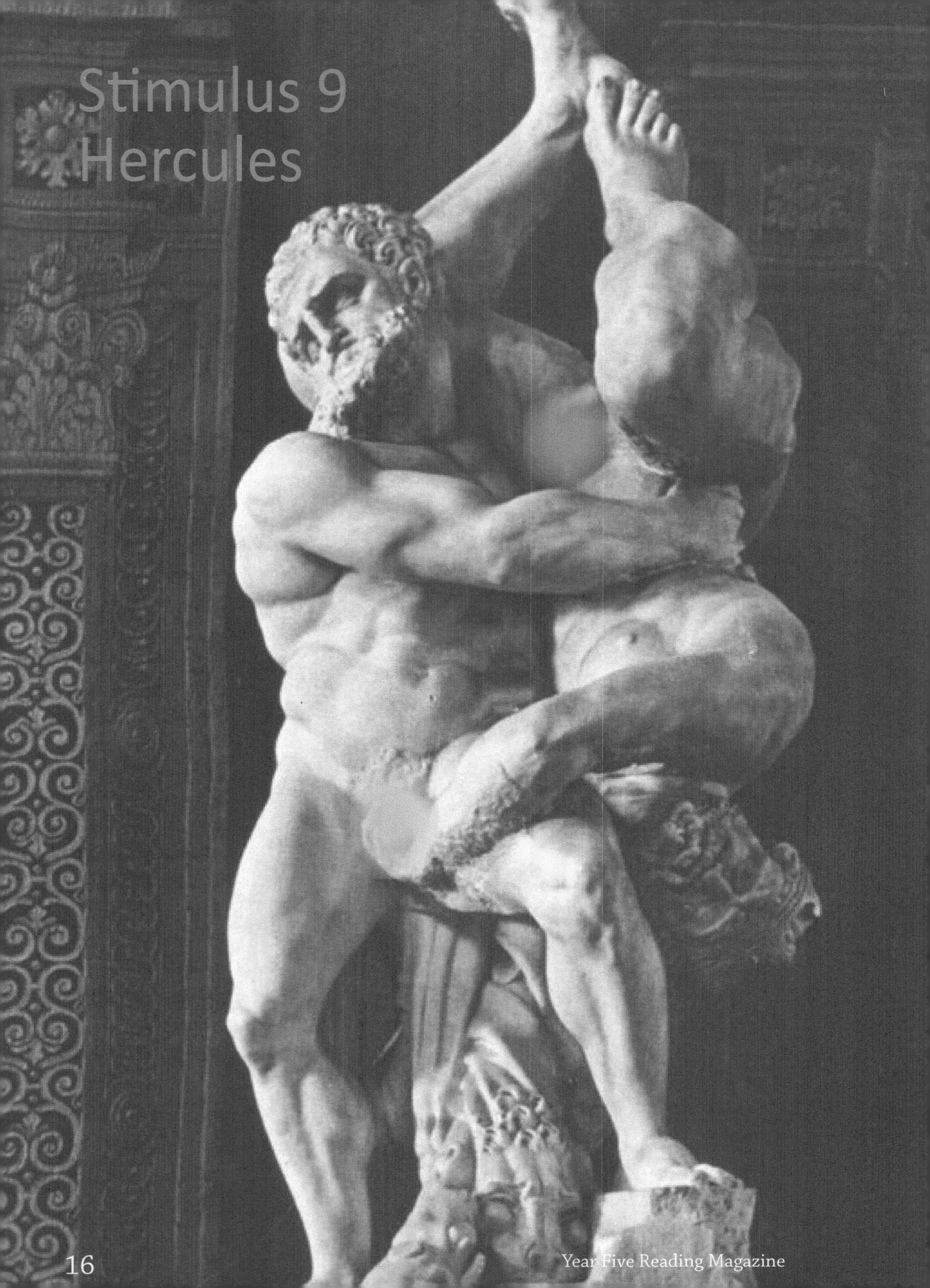

Hercules, a Greek hero, had seven labours to complete Here are the first two:

Labour One: The Nemean Lion

As his first Labor, Hercules was challenged to kill the Nemean lion. This was no easy feat, for the beast's parentage was supernatural and it was more of a monster than an ordinary lion. Its skin could not be penetrated by spears or arrows. Hercules blocked off the entrances to the lion's cave, crawled into the close confines where it would have to fight face to face and throttled it to death with his bare hands. Ever afterwards he wore the lion's skin as a cloak and its gaping jaws as a helmet.

Labour Two: The Hydra

Hercules was to seek out and destroy the monstrous and many-headed Hydra. The storytellers agree that the Hydra lived in the swamps of Lerna, but they seem to have had trouble counting its heads. Some said that the Hydra had eight or nine, while others claimed as many as ten thousand. One man warned Hercules, 'As soon as one head is beaten down or chopped off, two more grow in its place'.
Eventually Hercules chopped off the right head and won the battle because his friend helped him stop the heads growing back.

Stimulus 10: Jungle Escape

(an excerpt from the novel Kestrin's Jungle Adventures by Hansie Boer)

Kestrin could hear the hyena pack prowling at the entrance to the cave. At this stage the fire she had lit was keeping them at bay but with no wood left her chances of escape were small. She thought she would need all her jungle lore she had gathered from her years in the African jungle to get out of this dangerous predicament. Kestrin only wished her father, the Park Ranger, could have been here.

With no hope of getting home out the front she decided to take one branch from the fire and head to the back of the cave. She may get trapped but it seemed the only hope. As she grabbed the lit branch the pack howled in fury and Kestrin knew she had little time. As quickly as possible she moved past white bones of previous victims that were on the cave floor and into the blackness.

The light was dim but better than nothing as the cave narrowed and became damp and musty. It seemed to angle down for about one hundred metres before coming to an end. Kestrin looked around helplessly just as the flame flickered brightly. It must be a breeze she thought and searched with intensity. She could find nothing as the branch began to burn away to nothing. Suddenly she saw the smoke rise and looked up. A hole in the roof gave her hope as she heard the pack enter the cave with echoing wails

Habitat : The savannah or savanna is a plain made up of coarse grasses and scattered trees growth, mainly on the edges of the tropics where the rainfall is seasonal, as in eastern Africa. The animals that inhabit or live in this area are unique and most of the animals on the savanna have long legs or wings to be able to go on long migrations.

Living in the Savannah: Many savannah animals burrow under ground to avoid the heat or raise their young. The savannah is a perfect place for birds of prey as the wide, open plain provides them with a clear view of their prey, hot air updrafts keep them soaring, and there is the odd tree to rest on or nest in.

Animal Life: Some animals specific to the savannah are the African elephant, Grant's Zebra and the African Wild Dog. The African elephant is the largest land mammal on the planet and they eat huge amounts of vegetation. They live in groups of ten to fifteen animals and are never, never bothered by predators as they have thick grey skin and are very big.

Stimulus 12
Timmy to the Rescue

(an excerpt from the novel Timmy's Terrific Tales by Elizabeth Britannia)

Timmy and his two friends Roderick and Stephen were building a secret hideout in the Ancient Woods behind Windsor Hall. It was a great spot as they could walk around the forest or head down to the river for some boating or fishing. The boys were gathering fallen logs with which to build their hideaway and they began to get further into the woods.

'This is very hot work' said Roderick. The two other boys agreed.

'What about a swim in the river?' asked Timmy.

Fabulous', they yelled and headed for the river where the water was cool and still.

At the riverbank they paddled into the water and sat beneath the shade of an old elm tree. Roderick looked out over the green fields dotted with sheep toward Richman Manor. He thought it odd that an old truck was in the drive when the Richman family were in the south of France for the holidays.

'By gosh that's strange boys', he said. 'What could that truck be doing? Let's investigate.'

All the boys got dressed and headed over the little bridge toward the Manor. Sneaking around the old stables Timmy and his friends observed two horrible looking men filling the van with valuables. The boys knew they were burglars and had to do something. They discussed their plan of action and Timmy volunteered to steal the keys from the van when the men were inside.

He moved silently to the back of the van and crept around to the van door, reached in and grabbed the keys. Just then he heard a voice cry out, 'Hey you' and he ran for the forest.

Stimulus 13: Goldfish

Goldfish were first kept as pets by the Chinese but it was the Japanese who bred them to develop the types we have today.

Of course the goldfish was originally gold but now the colours are red, black and white.

Goldfish are very easy to keep and will survive well in a fish tank. They live for over ten years and come in ten varieties. Goldfish will eat flakes or pellets especially made for them and you can decorate the tank.

Stimulus 14

Blackbeard's Ghost

The pirate Blackbeard (real name: Edward Teach) was a tall man with a very long black beard that covered his face and extended down to his waist. For two years Blackbeard terrorized the sailors of the oceans, ambushing ships and stealing their cargo, and often attacking in the dim light of dawn or dusk when his pirate ship was most difficult to see.

In November of 1718, Blackbeard retreated to his favorite hideaway -- called Teach's Hole -- off Ocracoke Island. There, he hosted a pirate party with dancing and large bonfires. The party lasted for days, and eventually the government sent Lieutenant Robert Maynard of the Royal Navy, to go and capture Blackbeard. Maynard attacked Blackbeard in a terrible battle. Maynard pretended to lose the battle and when the pirates boarded the ship, Maynard and his men attacked them

Outnumbered, the pirates put up a good fight but eventually he was defeated. From then until now, Blackbeard's ghost has haunted Teach's Hole as a headless ghost. Sometimes according to the legend, people see a strange light coming from the shore of Ocracoke Island and know that it is "Teach's light". On nights that the ghost light appears, if the wind is blowing inland, you can still hear Blackbeard's ghost tramping up and down andcalling: 'Where's my head?'

Stimulus 15: Harmony Day

Harmony Day is celebrated on 21 March each year in Australia. It is organised by the Department of Immigration and Citizenship which is part of the Australian Government. Harmony Day celebrates the multicultural nature of our nation and promotes cultural diversity.

Community events and activities held to celebrate Harmony Day and schools also participate to help spread the word about different cultures living together. The message of Harmony Day is 'Everyone Belongs'. It's about getting together, joining in, respect for others and a sense of belonging for everyone.

The theme this year is 'Express Yourself'. This allows people the opportunity to share with others the importance of different cultures in every aspect of life. Join in Harmony Day events and help unite the nation. In your school you can help plan activities like a food day or games day.

Stimulus 16: Desert Mystery

(an excerpt from the novel *Sahara Journeys* by Sandra Leader)

Sandhill after sandhill greeted the struggling travellers as they plodded along hoping for respite. The small band that had survived the crash probably should have stayed with the plane wreck but had moved on hoping to find help or at least an oasis that would assist their survival. Now all seemed lost and Rocco thought that the five of them would perish out here in the heat without water that day.

He turned to look at the others who were following. Jemima and Tony, the young newlyweds, the journalist Toby Stevens and his photographer girlfriend, Stephanie looked like they were ready to fall down. Sun blistered faces and no conversation gave away how they felt. Rocco knew there had to be something up ahead from his many trips across the desert in the plane but it was very different at ground level. They hadn't seen a living thing for three days and now the water was gone hope was fading.

'I think it's over the next hill', Rocco said hopefully to spur them on but they just stared at him.

They continued to trudge listlessly but were startled by a breathy honking noise. Staring up into the sun they were face to face with a line of camels led by a young boy who jokingly called out, 'No pyramids here'.

They all smiled at this and knew they would be alright from this moment on. Relief seemed to surge through the group and more smiles broke out as they laughed.

Stimulus 17
FOOTBALL

THE WORLD GAME

By Special Reporter: Stephen Torres

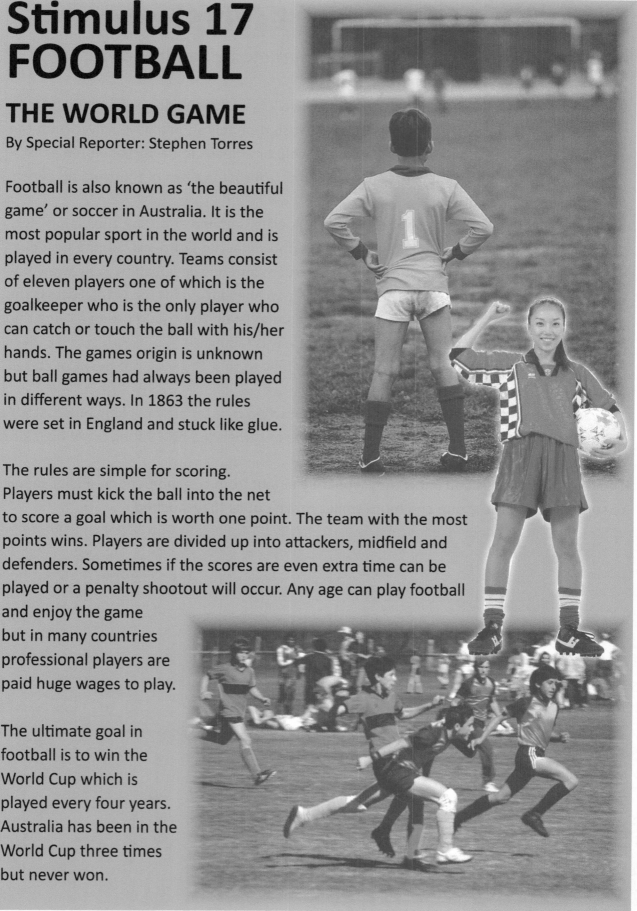

Football is also known as 'the beautiful game' or soccer in Australia. It is the most popular sport in the world and is played in every country. Teams consist of eleven players one of which is the goalkeeper who is the only player who can catch or touch the ball with his/her hands. The games origin is unknown but ball games had always been played in different ways. In 1863 the rules were set in England and stuck like glue.

The rules are simple for scoring. Players must kick the ball into the net to score a goal which is worth one point. The team with the most points wins. Players are divided up into attackers, midfield and defenders. Sometimes if the scores are even extra time can be played or a penalty shootout will occur. Any age can play football and enjoy the game but in many countries professional players are paid huge wages to play.

The ultimate goal in football is to win the World Cup which is played every four years. Australia has been in the World Cup three times but never won.

Stimulus 18: Man Overboard

(an excerpt from the novel *Smuggler's Cove* by Scurvy Knave)

Richard's father hid silently behind the rocky outcrop on the point. He didn't know Richard had secretly scampered out behind him and was also watching from a safe distance. Richard wanted to see his dad catch the smugglers at work that night. His father was the local magistrate and had been having some trouble with criminals in the area. The night was blustery and the wind whipped up the waves.

After what seemed like a long wait a light shone through the salt spray and waves. The smugglers boat was heading for the beach and it looked in trouble as the waves crashed over the bow. Richard's dad headed down toward the beach to trap them onshore and Richard followed more closely as the bad weather made visibility poor.

Next instant he saw his father run toward the beach and call out to a man standing on the water's edge. Richard followed quickly and caught his father yelling at the man. The man stammered someone was overboard and couldn't swim. Grabbing a rope Richard's father dived into the surf and headed for the noise the man was making in the water. Richard could only stand on the beach and hope things would be alright.

The rope was coming to an end when he noticed the cowardly smuggler had run off. He grabbed the rope and when he heard his father over the roar of the surf began to pull with all his energy. When he saw the two bodies in the rough water he waded out and helped drag the smuggler in with his father. The man looked sick but was still alive. Richard's father was puffing hard from his efforts and was dripping wet.

Sample Questions

Read the following story and answer the four questions on the next page. You will find these questions similar to the types you will find in this book and the examination.

URBAN LEGENDS

THE LEGEND:

It was once a common among parents holidaying in Florida to bring back baby alligators for their children to have as pets. These infant alligators eventually grew up and became to big to handle. This caused a disposal problem. Their desperate owners flushed them down the toilet or released them into the sewers/ stormwater to get rid of them.

Some of these speedily disposed-of creatures managed to survive and breed in the dark city sewer system, so the story goes, producing colonies of giant, albino alligators beneath the streets of New York. Their babies thrive down there to this day, completely hidden except for the rare scary encounter between sewer gator and underground worker.

Is this the truth or just an urban myth? What do you think?

1 Why did parents bring back baby alligators?
   - ☐ to put in the sewer
   - ☐ to donate to the zoo
   - ☐ to keep as children's pets
   - ☐ to remind them of Florida

2 Another word for ''infant' in the passage might be?
   - ☐ crocodile
   - ☐ baby
   - ☐ reptile
   - ☐ small

3 What colour did the underground alligators turn?
   - ☐ albino
   - ☐ brown
   - ☐ green
   - ☐ lemon

4 Write the numbers 1 to 4 in the spaces to show the order events happen in the legend
   - _____ alligators bred underground
   - _____ alligators arrive from Florida
   - _____ alligators are dumped when growing
   - _____ alligators meet underground workers

Answers
1. to keep as children's pets
2. baby
3. albino
4. alligators arrive from Florida, alligators dumped when growing, alligators bred underground, alligators met underground workers.

READING MAGAZINE YEAR 5 is a supplement to
YEAR 5 READING NAPLAN*-FORMAT PRACTICE TESTS with answers

© Alfred Fletcher 2010   Published by Coroneos Publications 2010   ISBN 978-1-921565-48-9